seedtime

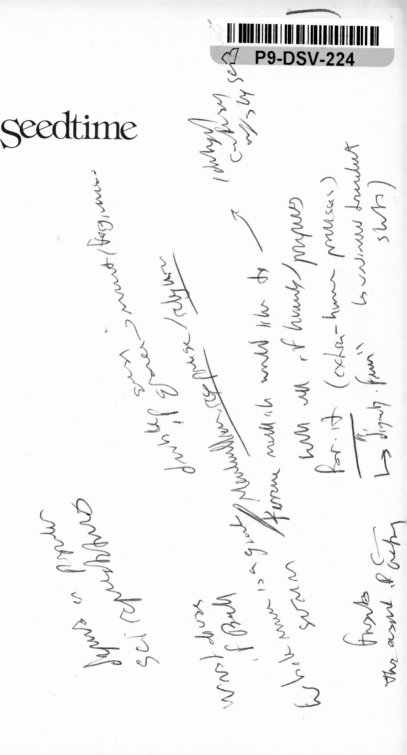

Philippe Jaccottet

Seedtime

(La Semaison)

EXTRACTS FROM THE NOTEBOOKS 1954–1967

Prose selections translated by André Lefevere,
verse translated by Michael Hamburger

A NEW DIRECTIONS BOOK

Manufactured in the United States of America
First published clothbound and as New Directions Paperbook 428 in 1977
Published simultaneously in Canada by McClelland & Stewart, Ltd.

Library of Congress Cataloging in Publication Data

Jaccottet, Philippe.
    Seedtime = (La semaison).

    I. Hamburger, Michael. II. Title.
PQ2670.A225S413   1977   848'.9'1409   76–45640
ISBN 0–8112–0636–x
ISBN 0–8112–0637–8 pbk.

New Directions Books are published for James Laughlin
by New Directions Publishing Corporation,
333 Sixth Avenue, New York 10014

1956

OCTOBER

The reeds: how their velvety ears burst, allow the slow escape of a stream of seeds, a crop, in the most absolute *silence*. A woman giving birth: moans of pain, blood. In absolute silence, sweet, irresistibly slow, the plant bursts and scatters itself on the mercy of the wind.

1958

MAY/MAJORCA

Evening, orchards of almond trees, their black trunks. High palm bushes like a multitude of green fans. Pine forests and dark mountains beyond. Or else the blue of the sea between the trunks and the green, but the word blue is not good enough, too soft, one is almost tempted to say black, and that, too, would be wrong. Concentrated, piled-up blue, thick like a wall. No opening, in any case. A wealth of blue. Nothing glitters, nothing moves. No patches either. Intense, but calm, motionless, opaque, deep. A blue presence as strong as the earth, as heavy, as rich, but one, no details. The whole landscape too, for that matter, as seen from inside a forest, almost motionless, but airy, light and strong at the same time, calm and vibrating, powerful but not ostentatious, more vertical than horizontal.

The plants old, hard, thorny, but not meagre as in Provence. A quiet wealth, full of strength, no cries, but no murmur either. Not the slightest trace of a river or running water, or water welling up, and yet no drought. Heat as constant and powerful, but quietly fanned by the sea.

A congregation of strong presences brought together, rich and calm. A powerful serenity. Broad base. A flash of authority with a voice never strained.

Luminous monuments, vast wind-swept domains. No bombast. Gabrieli brass. Gold maybe, no jewels.

Houses are just storage rooms here, in this season, full of shadow, small forts against the armies of the sun, water-castles, cool battlements. Archers all around, breastplates, flags. A great clanging of armour over the sea. An image, possible at any given moment, but one must go beyond, erase.

Wealth, power beyond the walls: strength, constant and motionless, calm authority of space, mechanical sound of the sea, one could almost forget one's burdens, infinitely light.

The forest full of sound.

The rocks. They are like the pages of a dossier, here and there, pressed hard by a giant hand, like the pages of a book under the press, before they are stitched together. More often in great disorder, hollowed out by the sea in all directions, pierced, turned upside down, broken. Between the moving glitter of the sea and the calm fertility of the soil.

Plants that stand up to the wind, that can shudder only with their tops.

Clash of a stubborn power and a power completely motionless, lowly, immensely mute: on that border line rises a white flame, a combustion of drops of water blossoming, abrupt, withered at once. The way time uses us, and our labours flash for a moment under its strokes.

2

NOVEMBER

Trails of fire in the grass before snow
like the flaring in the western sky before night
the soul's leap to attention before death.
a fighter who dresses up in his wounds

*

Above the chasm of that desperate zeal,
those efforts, those smiles, those labours,
the slow raising of monuments, of pavillions
above the chasm those battles, those wounds,
so much effort, violence, passion,
those minute calculations, those monstrous army trucks,
those explosions and crumblings
a whirlwind of leaves more or less gilded
above the bottomless depth
and yet . . .
          of that battle between the chasm and its prey,
however condemned the prey, however triumphant the chasm,
I cannot say yet who will be the winner,
if winner there is, if one can speak of victory,
if that imperious image is not false,
if my glance in picking it up has not already
gone too far, if saying battle I have not
predicted peace, prepared its coming . . .
O secret of battle, visible in a flight of leaves,
visible in the abyss but never deciphered,
O black I give to my fist as a torch,
as a woman's hair and dark falcon in the blackness

*

Stars veiled by trees, by mist,
winter's face.

DECEMBER

Just before eight, when the sky is completely overcast, the world is brown only, a table of earth. A lamp lit in the street here, yellow like a sun without rays, there a gilded door opens, a shadow looks, long, at the weather that will come to the garden.

*

The mobile, translucid constellations of rain on the windows, they are only veils on the march, seen from afar, curtains closing. The panting, irregular wind from the south; the wind from the north, mechanical.

1959

FEBRUARY

Frozen snow in the morning.

At night, after a day of uninterrupted snow, a landscape white, brown and black, seldom seen here. That weight on the trees, so light, as if we looked at them through gauze. A joy of childhood over the whole village: old men throw snowballs.

OCTOBER

Gilded light in the cold air this evening. How quickly it departs from the trees and rises up to the clouds, carried away by the wind. Dead acacia leaves in the garden, pale yellow, the first to fall, abundant on the ground every day. The leaves of the ebony tree turn with more emphasis, slow and complex, while the fruit ripens. The peach tree, still green, grows lighter. The vine is almost completely stripped bare, old, sick. Colors of autumn daisies or small chrysanthemums that match the season so well. A bush pink from top to bottom.

Now gold turns to pink, and the green of fields, trees, grows darker; change from yellow to blue green. Arrows of the wind. The road has the colour of water, slate grey. A few clouds look like smoke, already. Intimacy of light in the room, on the white paper that has grown almost pink in its turn. Books, objects in a sheath of shadow. The sound of the wind and words; nothing else.

Night will soon make writing without a lamp impossible. Day lives on the highest peak of the sky only. We turn our backs on the sun.

Purple clouds, lilac. Paper almost blue. A fire that goes out. I can't see the words any more, almost.

Still gold on the other side, but the blue wins in the east. Gold-silver. Day-night.

Raise the jewel above the night once more, above the abyss. Dream-jewel: learned and musical in one, solid and mute, vast and hidden. Models: Hölderlin, Leopardi, a few poems by Baudelaire.

Movement is easy in the infinite. Birds. Other examples, the most beautiful maybe, in Dante: *Dolce color d'oriental zaffiro* . . . But no Thomism left, these days, no sacred numbers, etc. Loneliness, resignation, threats, and the sapphire so much sweeter.

Reservations (absurd, of course): Leopardi's thoughts and allegories, the tension in Hölderlin, Baudelaire's poses.

Something else ought to be tried, maybe, where light and heavy, reality and mystery, detail and space enter into harmony, not peaceful, but alive. Grass, air. Glimpses infinitely fragile and beautiful—as of a flower, a gem, a golden artifact—placed in the extraordinary immensity. Stars and night. Discourse vast and liquid, airy, in which gems of language take their place, discreetly. It appears in the mist, at times, far away. Or else you perform some menial task, and suddenly remember the depths of space and time.

Naïve questions. Why is this beautiful and not that? A direct experience, often, while you are working: this is a lie and that is not, or less so. An order, therefore, hope?

Leopardi maintains that beauty is an illusion and a decoy: but how come it exists, how come he gave in to its power, how come he served it so well? How can you deny that it says something essential, how can you put it on the same level with common lies? Is so much doubt necessary? Even if everything frustrates and exploits us, by and large.

*

It is by no means certain that the modern era, with all its negative components—an enormous mass that darkens the sky —does not have a happy message for us as well: we are children of time and we are given all things through time; all opposites are not to be dissolved and we must not, and cannot, escape from contradiction; our only task is not to let one of its terms grow stronger than the other.

Our condition is so strange because it does not include substantial progress, because we never come near to any definitive answer. We know we shall not find an answer, and yet we go on asking questions, because that is the essence of our nature. Strange also that nothing religious or philosophical, for instance, is ever experienced for others; the experience must be repeated, lived again, to be of any value; and so one must always start again.

Hence the irritating feeling of marking time: *Seinesgleichen geschieht*, says Musil.

The same holds true, for example, for the intuition that is the origin of many poems. Somebody says, more or less, "I then felt as if the order of the world had been revealed to me" or else "I understood the language of the birds" or "The veil that is normally between us and reality was rent" (which is also a theme in fairy tales). These are, indubitably, *facts*, of course, experiences (you can treat them as lies, but they happen, nonetheless)—an experience of that kind can take on various forms, but the result is always the same. It has happened ever since man first appeared on earth, and you can find hundreds of examples in mystic, philosophical or purely literary texts. You could object that such an experience is a mirage, but what makes such a mirage possible, and why could it not have a meaning, even as a mirage?

That mirage, or that intuition, revelation or dream, sets an order against disorder, a fulness against the void, and wonder, enthusiasm, hope against disgust. Is it possible to believe that man's obsession with order in so many different fields could be totally devoid of sense? And do we not have the duty, or at least the right, to listen to that very deep, irresistible nostalgia within ourselves, as if it really said something important and true? Is it not narrow-minded to refuse to believe in the enigma that attracts and enlightens us? Is it more equitable to believe only in skeletons, ruins? Would life not, indeed, flow into us if we grew more supple? Let us remain faithful to our immediate experience, rather than be eager to listen to whatever may contradict it from outside.

*

Go on all the same, start from uncertainty. Take nothing for granted, for is not all that is established paralysed? Uncertainty is the motor, shadow the source. I walk because I have nowhere to stay, I speak because I don't know, to prove that I am still alive. Stammering, I have not been struck down yet. What I have done is no use even if it were appreciated, accepted as a completed phase. *Magician of insecurity the poet*, Char, absolutely right. If I breathe it is because I still don't know. *Moving earth, horrible, exquisite*, Char again. No explanations, but the right pronunciation.

But how do you start again? That is the whole problem. On what twisting, indirect road. On what absence of roads? You start from nakedness, weakness, doubt. You find help only in forgetting what has been done, in despising what is done and applauded, advised or hinted at for writers today.

7

Defy the levelling of souls above all else. Not the castoffs of princes, of unfrocked knights, but their pride, their tact. There is no poetry without reserve. Of that at least I am certain, and strong in that conviction for lack of more strength. But no castles: streets, rooms, roads, our life.

*

Autumn, rainy fire, old fire, pyre. Old iron, wood and mist. Rust, ashes. Ashy dawn, consummated, party over, decorations torn, washed out. Armed fog marching across gardens and fields. The ploughshare of the cold comes closer and glistens. The shadow, upright, ploughs backwards.

. . . And yet I have seen them again, the fields, the trees, the valleys as they always were in this season when a beautiful day establishes itself between two spells of wind or rain. I have found it again, the feeble light of autumn on the trunks of oaks, and that kind of gilded humming under their leaves, supported by those strong arms or black twisted columns; the yellow poplars too, motionless along the invisible water; and the curves of the earth almost unveiled; and the tables of rock among the low trees, the thorny bushes where dark green and rust red mingle; and the glittering ploughland; pigeons fly up with the sound of applause, of washing in the wind, and two are whiter than all the others that write the pure line of their flight on the blue of the sky. The clouds of the horizon have hardly veiled the sun when all becomes dark and the cold passes over the whole landscape like a scythe. Smokes rises up far, far away.

To speak with that void in your heart, against it. Growths of acacias on the white, almost blue of the sky. Burn dead leaves, tear out weeds, content, maybe, to do just that.

Those growths with their pale leaves, slender. The beginning of winter.

*

Fed on the dark, I speak
and chewing the cud from a meagre pasture of shades,
poor, weak, leaning back on the ruins of rain
I rely on that which I cannot doubt,
on doubt, and inhabiting the uninhabitable, look
and begin again to mutter against death
at death's dictation. Crumbling I persevere
at seeing, I see this crumbling shine
and all the distance of the earth
all the depths of the age vaguely
lit up, an intenable comfort,
a wing under the cover of grey clouds.
The dark opens my eyes
and the drawing close of the impossible deep in the day,
this invasion of ashes deep in myself, victorious,
insolent, fierce, do not silence me,
dictate new arguments to me, in despair
of a cause, and I grope amid old words
amid the ruins of old verses,
with nothing to uphold me or guide me
but the power of error,
but the dark that does not speak and carries no lamp.

*

So at the end of a story too long
when there is nothing left but broken columns and rats' nests
    in the banners,
must we really despair?
Isn't it so many lies given back to their brittleness?
Let me lean back on the column of the rain
to celebrate the wind's triumph.

*

Still upheld by the interminable gloom
and butted in the back by brutal night
at the limit of my strength in this November dawn
I see the shaft of the cold advancing, flaring

and behind it in a light grown brighter
the dark is ploughing

*

I speak for the dark that moves off at the end of the day
or isn't it rather the dark that sings as it moves off,
the stride that bearing the dark away to the fields
speaks with all the comfort of distance?
What air is this more melodious than air,
if not the tearing itself and the distance of earth
that murmurs lovingly, if not the hours
that of their passing make a chain of words?

Those who vanish do not weep but sing.
Trees, houses, flowers disintegrate by turns
as far as the roads where the dark moves at the same
            pace always
with half-closed eyes fixed on the arrowhead.
And there, where the dark at last goes out of sight
hardly higher than she so yielding and vanished now,
rises a mountain's breath.

*

Into your hand that will not touch again
either the rough or the smooth of earth I slip
this leaf, hardly a wing, hardly an arrow a little bright
to serve as guide, or as lamp, or as obol;
against the chasm's voracity it has
the power of the invisible only. What it says
to ruin's thunder is no more than the defiance
of that which cannot be seen or believed or confirmed
directly or through an image, and of which nonetheless
I make you a gift. What it conveys is like
a faint track in the snow, of a movement
attesting there is not a smile but it fades
that there is not a smile born but under the hatchet
of time.

*

How will you stand up in this dilapidation of worlds
this crumbling, storm, invasion of infinities
their triumph amid our ruins advances
between two ranks of the prostrate, carrying trophies
      of stars.
Of our dreams it will leave none standing
of our places of refuge

Where should your foot rest, and your heart look
for nourishment? The world slips, the seasons
remove themselves, and the purest lines are blurred.
The joints of words crack, some of them go down,
others grow remote, but the very base
and distance itself are no longer grasped.

Will there be tears limpid enough
to clear a road for us through these lands?
But it is no longer a matter of lands, roads,
of nights to get through, if now there is
no land, no day, no expanse?
If the source of tears has dried up?
If the wind, not even the wind, if the storm
or rather the storm within the storms
carries off the least of arguments
and the mouth that speaks them, and the faces
that inclined towards its comfort, and comfort,
carries off the carrying off
as though a fire were to turn against itself
to consume the memory of fire, the name of fire,
even the possibility of fire,
if the sea withdraws from the sea, and the worlds,
all the worlds roll up like tents at the breaking of a camp?
No one before us will have thought a blinder thought
or had a closer view of a vaster disorder.

*

I see the sign of gold on the lime tree.

So too the sacrifice, in the Odyssey, of a cow with her horns painted in gold.

What reaches us because it burns itself out, disappears. Burning wood. Death alone has ever spoken in me, through my mouth. All poetry is a voice for death. That our decay may praise, celebrate. That our defeat may shine, trumpet.

I would be without eyes if I were not walking towards the end.

Birds wheel around or fly like arrows, nobody sees you except the dying, who burn themselves out, who slowly fall into dust.

The eyes and the voice of the destroyed.

*

1960

FEBRUARY

"Someone will place in your hand a seed
so that even after your hand's destruction
nothing will have been taken from you or broken."

Words spoken for ignorance of the sequel,
for walking in doubt and in affliction,
confided by folly to the unknown.

Words imprecise, however, or false,
when there can be no question of a gift or seed
nor of destruction, nor of anything breaking,

When it is a question of defying the grave,
of breaking reason and human semblance
as a prison too narrow and too precise.

Word ventured so as to be more brave
so as to give oneself a bearing more grave
and to clear the air for such a seed.

*

Wood differs from the earth only by its form. All things
have the colour of the earth, almost pink, up to where the
snow has pitched camp. I set a fire of old wood against the
snow, against the snowy buds of the almond tree. Prelude to
spring. A few words thrown away, light.

Here I must convey a vast expanse of air, mobility, glitter,
animation, above the immovable, the old, the immemorial,
hardly decorated with wreaths of flowers, crowned with laurel.
A country laid bare, yet elsewhere, in winter, snow comes to
hide the soil, the foundations are more easily visible. But the
rock is not heavy: it is weighty, severe, it reminds you of war-
riors, invincible, but without grandiloquence or dash, a power,
true, silent—that allows, and purifies the joyful animation of
the air above.

The almond tree in bloom, the peach tree, compared to
cherry trees, apple trees, prune trees, the pride of the north.
There is overabundance in those foamy globes above the high
grass, in bloom itself, almost ostentatious. But this is the ut-
most in delicacy, a flower in the air, still fresh, on naked
branches, the naked earth, both almost of the same colour,
that combination of the ruddy and the exquisite, and as if of
old age with most brittle youth, one of the wonders of the
world. Show it, grasp it, dust and flower, wood and silk. What
is there to say about that pink, that white? The pink of the
carnation is of another kind and the word pink has many over-
tones one should suppress here, especially the erotic ones.

Because we are facing the purest.

In the same way even the wounds of trees don't look
repulsive, frightening, like the wounds of men or animals.
Strange. Where does the horrible begin? Similarly, neither

wood nor dead leaves scare, repulse people. Horror of blood. Sap that runs is just a tear. That is why all connections between the human and the vegetal are uncertain—in spite of a thousand traditional metaphors. Novalis: *The infinitely receding world of flowers.*

*

The mountain always appears, with a last cap of snow, above the road to Rebavas, like something Greek, the nest of a great white owl, a small banner or a Tibetan thong. High spot in the light air, white bird above the trees without leaves.

Or the elbow of the river in the distance, at the bottom of the slope, hardly green: you see a colour of clear green water—the colour of some precious stones (jade, opal)—and one or two lines of living foam across to indicate its rapid motion as if arrested—the abundant water of the end of winter—and on the banks the naked trees, their smooth trunks, of a grey hardly grown yellow or pink in the feeble light, their branches ascending, straight—as opposed to the twisted, knotty trees that live among rocks. A place of brittle ascension, the branches of mist, so different from groups, augural circles of oaks covered with ivy, with their black force, their chains, their heavy bars, containing, defending who knows what austerity, what stone lifted, well or tomb. Circles, solemn, grave assemblies around a silence—and the hoopoes and gallinules live in the branches; places to stay, to wait, motionless, with sovereign resolve; whereas all things pass along the river, water, smoke, lane under the light arch of smoke, shining road.

Like two lives, two possible thoughts: one knotty, attentive, meditative and tied to the night, to the stone, druidic, bent over the mouth of the earth; the other lively, light, almost insolent or agile, along the sparkling thread of days.

Almond trees, foam, snow, summit of coolness, luminous crests, swans . . .

*

Days soft already in the morning, luminous, with the first movements of the birds.

MARCH

Pass under arches of vapour
in the haze of riverside trees
follow the sign of foam on jade
colour of the swelling of late winter waters.
The soil on both sides of that passage is fed by water
and wears a precocious green. The rising of a breeze,
and passing through of a fresh breeze.
Beam cast by the mirror of ice to the mirror of the sea
according to the ground's changing slope.
Light flow, sparkling from one end to the other,
and the more so where stones oppose it.
Another lesson to be learnt from the world.

*

Immemorial tomb or monument
with no other decoration than tough ivy
a garland that says to the passer-by
bronze of war or leafage of night

At the foot, offered by an intimate source
to the man who comes and the man who goes
a bowl of honey, a bell jar of milk.

Or:

Immemorial monument or great urn
with no other decoration than tough ivy
a garland suggesting to the man who passes
bronze of war or leafage of night.

To him whom that rock celebrates
as to him who living comes to it,
the primrose offers its honey bowl,
the snowdrop its bell jar of milk.

*

Night, cloudy, dark, without depth, with flaps or twisted fringes, whitish slopes, as if somebody held a lamp behind the clouds in certain spots in heaven, more to frighten or lead astray than to give light, show the way. The humid curtains of a theatre where nothing good will happen. Pale. Above the familiar landscape I know by heart, almost, that space suddenly unknown, that sky by Greco. And yet this is only smoke and beyond it the whole chiselled geometry is intact, of knots tied by the winds, the troubled breath of forests and the earth in spring, wet straw.

The peach tree in bloom: an impression of crowds, swarms, humming in the budding which has always struck me as the clearest feature of early spring. Of silent explosion, too. But it is particularly the multiplicity, the multitude that strikes you. And then the first flower open under the rain, like a pink star. Constellation of the peach tree. With the colour of dawn. Peach tree, constellation of dawn.

Observer of the earthly zodiac, of a galaxy arrested in its motion in a garden. It will soon be the acacia's turn, I haven't forgotten, I would not have thought it so lavish. Perfumes, whiteness, night of May or June, the shortest of the year.

Wheat fields, mirrors scarred by wrinkles, waves, shudders. The spirit does not halt its course over this land.

Rain slanted, changing, passing or fleeing. Noise of a machine, undefined, maybe in the fields. Days still almost cold, malicious. The sound of cars is also like that of a machine, a tool that would go down into the matter of the air to pierce it.

Short words like a quick rain. Like the lines it leaves on the window for a moment, brilliant, starry, and yet each pearl, each drop has its knot of shadow. Behind the star of tears, the grass a bit greener, still, and an analogous multitude in the nest of the trees. A blue smoke, like what is far away.

*

Draw near again, Destroyer,
Let me see your face and let it counsel me breaking.
But it is I who advance and I think I see him before me
Under the mask perfumed with carnival violets.
Is it not urgent to know him before he breaks my bones?
But he takes the question out of my mouth,
he disarms me by stripping me like almond petals
and the more I search the more he drives me astray,
the more I want to defy him the larger he grows and escapes
    me.
Already I give up earthly cares to contemplate only him
when he pits himself against beauty, when he demolishes walls.
In him I saw the source of day
and in him I must learn to recognise at the same time
him who poisons water.
I must grasp as one invisible reality
source and ashes, lips and a dead rat.
I praised him too soon for the daylight he pours out,
his revenge is to appear unnameable under that brightness,
refusing me a peace at so cheap a price,
regaining vigour under his exquisite guise.

*

A gentleness like that of light
when the sun, going down in the west, makes it longer and
    more golden,
a breath of gentleness given to near things
out of compassion for their approaching fall,
a gentleness defying the enemy's coarseness,
a firm patience in face of torturing time,
the gift of gentleness condemned on every side
inexhaustibly, by an inexhaustible answer.

*

Noon over, light is bruised,
owns itself troubled and no longer has any task
but to impose an order on its dissolution.

*

You try to grasp the Completely Other. How do you explain that you look for him and fail to find him, but go on looking. The infinite is the *breath* that gives us life. The dark is a breath. God is a breath. You cannot get hold of him. Poetry is the word that breath feeds and carries, hence its power over us.

All poetic activity devotes itself to reconcile, or at least bring closer, the bounded and the boundless, the clear and the obscure, the breath and the form. That is why the poem brings us back to our centre, our central preoccupation, a metaphysical question. The breath pushes, mounts, unfolds, vanishes; it gives us life and eludes us, we try to grasp it without smothering it. We invent a language for it in which the rigorous and the vague come together, where measure does not prevent movement from continuing, but reveals it, that is does not let it lose itself completely.

It is possible that beauty is born when the bounded and the boundless become visible at the same time, that is to say, when you can see forms, but you can also guess that they don't say all, that they are not reduced to themselves, that they leave its share to what cannot be grasped. There is no beauty, at least for our eyes, in what cannot be grasped alone, and there is also no beauty in forms without depth, completely revealed, unfolded. But the combinations of the bounded and the boundless are themselves infinite in number, hence the variety of art. The boundless is strongly present in Rembrandt; in Ingres there is almost nothing but forms, and his art is poor, in spite of his great technique. One could say that the boundless is domesticated, muffled in Chardin, in Braque, like fire in a lantern. That cannot be the *whole* of art either. In the *Divina Commedia* the boundless is what imposes its shape on the bounded, everything is ordained by a grandiose design legitimized by a truly great vision; a stupendous intellectual effort to give form to the Absolute.

Even if man goes on pushing back his limitations, the

boundless is not reduced in size because otherwise it would not be boundless. There lies the mistake of a number of moderns, who look on the boundless in quantitative terms and who believe that man gains on it if he successfully undertakes to walk the skies. But the sky has been an image of the boundless only for so long as the sky itself seemed boundless, inaccessible. Nothing that is visible seems safe from man's power at the present moment; but the truly invisible has not changed, nor diminished, nor weakened in any way; it has only found its real nature, which is without images. God is truly spirit now, and absolutely out of the reach of all images, except negative ones. God cannot even be called God now, any more. He will no longer be taken for a king.

That is no reason to believe that there are no more forms, limitations, visible, finite things. But one must pay more attention to the use of words. We would, indeed, do well to ask ourselves if God has ever been more powerful than today, now that his death has been proclaimed.

*

Strange, all this.

I have watched the face of the night and the gems with which it adorns its own receding. Sultaness not to be possessed, the lower part of the face under the veil of lunar mist, beauty burnt, charred, fire no hand can grasp.

*

Inside, outside. What do we mean by inside? Where does outside end? Where does inside begin? The white page belongs to the outside, but the words written on it? The whole of the white page is in the white page, therefore outside myself, but the whole word is not in the word. That is to say there is the sign I write down, and its meaning on top of that; the word has first been in me, then it leaves me and, once written, it looks like strapwork, like a drawing in the sand; but it keeps something hidden, to be perceived only by the mind. It is the mind that is inside, and the outside is all the mind seizes on, all that affects, touches it. In itself it has neither shape, nor weight, nor colour; but it makes use of shapes, weights, colours, it plays with them, according to certain rules. All that is surprising. It is not the heart that is inside, in fact the only real inside is precisely what this localisation cannot be properly applied to. Inside ourselves there are organs, and inside those organs the inside of those organs and one doesn't go beyond that: that inside is still outside, something visible, in a way, something with a shape, weight, colour.

But the inside we set against the outside (when we speak about the inner life, for instance) is by no means inside, by no means outside, or rather inside in a certain sense only: like waves sent and received, it circulates, and materializes if it hits the outside. *Deus intimior meo* (?) God more "inside" than I myself, absolutely inside, absolutely not outside. God inside the word, Breath. Those who manipulate words are closer to God; it is their duty, therefore, to respect the word because it carries the breath, instead of hiding, codifying, extinguishing it. A passage for words, an opening left for the breath. That is why we like valleys, rivers, roads, the air. They give us intimations of that breath. Nothing is accomplished. One must feel that exhalation, and feel that the world is only the transitory shape of the breath.

Maybe rhythmical speech is a more or less successful imitation of that breath. It hints at a power that expands, ascends, while bowing to an order, a shape; a power which does not, therefore, spend, squander itself. Everything is a hiatus in the breathing, provisional, a moment's rest for the divinity which breathes for ever. The whole universe like a breath, suspended. As when the wind falls in the garden and starts up again, and things change; but nothing is lost; the divinity breathes for ever.

The invisible power, the heart of the world breathes again: trees are born, mountains; but their precariousness, their movement, their nature: transitory, in suspense, is apparent to the alert eye.

*

The boundless should not be stronger than the bounded:

that is the curse of art today. Poetics harmful to poetry, or, in any case, dangerous for it. We know too well what we ought to do. And yet also be true to what is our truth, and keeps us from imitating the old masters. All things always start anew, from ifs and doubts, new difficulties. There, too, is hope: in darkness, in the impossible. Impossible to deny that point of departure, even if it is like a trap which seems to allow no escape.

*

The poem in long and regular lines no doubt presupposes a rather deep and peaceful breath, which I have lost, or which I no longer possess naturally, all the time. Things, instants made solemn, agreement, harmony, happiness. But how do you proceed from a number of "notes towards a poem" to the poem itself? The voice falls back too soon. There is an interesting problem in the opposition between the poem-instant (Ungaretti's *Allegria*) and the poem-discourse that has always been mine, like a slightly solemn short story, psalmodied just above the earth.

How do you convey feelings, how do you establish a fragile equilibrium, something not unlike a glass column, or even a column made of water, resting on the void? You lean on the poem itself, a brittle support, half treacherous. It shines and crashes: a waterfall heard in the night. The poem confused with its object.

APRIL

Still spring: the mixture of warm and cold. Gusts of warmth in the air that is still cold, like balls of wool rolling in it. Wind from the south or the west. Shadows passing above the trees, the gardens. Irises, tulips, stockflowers, periwinkles.

Trembling, the rose leaves beat their wings against the wall. The perfume of the iris.

The trees take on their burdens already, the banner, already, of the chestnut trees. You would like to catch their beginnings, and it will soon be too late. The oaks themselves are burgeoning.

Those banners trembling against the walls. I can see the transition from spring to summer more clearly in the garden today, it closes in on itself and covers itself little by little, changes into a pavilion or grotto of leaves, whereas in winter all is open: iron lattices, lattices of naked branches, and the dusty earth, and the stones, and only a few grey plants, lavender, lavender cotton, shepherd's purse. Grey, brown, white, wood, stone, iron, soil. Then comes the short moment—March —when white or pink butterflies move their wings between those naked, elementary materials, a moment of short fire and light snow as if arrested in the air above the dust, and the greenery is already reborn, following an unchangeable order, like a humming that takes hold now here, now there; the greenery of privets and climbing roses, with that of the peach tree and the almond tree, then the ebony tree, brilliant, almost yellow, then the fig tree; later still, very light and trembling the acacia, finally the lime tree. It isn't much, yet, the miracle is the fluttering of the rose leaves against the warm old stones, the leaves barely heavier than their shadow, and hard to distinguish from it, like a perpetual animation against the old calm of the wall, like a half-whispered conversation. But I remember all that comes later—especially in May, before the long dry heat—when space closes in on itself and covers itself, bends without ever being crushed, becomes a house of leaves and flowers, the best place to hide from the vast expanse.

*

To speak of a vanishing power, follow a poetry fled. Faith and challenge.

*

Desperate beauty of words, desperate defense of the impossible, of what all things contradict, deny, undermine, or wither. Every instant like the first and the last word, the first and the last poem, embarrassed, heavy, without force and without veracity, brittle, stubborn, persevering fountain; once more at night its sound against death, mischief, folly; once more its freshness, its limpidity against drivel. Once more the star out of its sheath.

*

The side I take now is that of the impossible
and my aging hand, I dedicate it once more
to the target always receding,
to arrows so quick that flight gilds them with fire.
In my undoing, only for gold now I speak
and, a near-nothing, for the vastness of space,
and, vile mould, for the spheres of the birds of prey,
and, straw, for the strongest wind and fire.

Everything breaks, everything wrinkles, everything is
     defeated,
we are born to see a falling and a bleeding,
to call us foetal is to flatter us,
but I who crumble shall make the daylight reign.

*

Again, once more, tonight, that vain
and desperate murmuring against that which feeds it,
word fathered by death, against death,
at once engendered and destroyed by death,
perpetual and impotent humming of small flies
against the decay of flesh
and the overhanging splendour of day.

*

A conversation of leaves on the stone wall,
not much longer shall we speak to the sun.
Our backs against that warm slab we laugh,
after that there is nothing left but the dark and
     the leaf's name . . .

MAY

Acacia in bloom at night: perfumed waterfall of honey. In perfect harmony with the first trillers of the birds, the moon, the flute of the owls. White rose bush, crown or diadem. Clear expanse, without weight or density.

*

All was grey dust save a little fire
and the oriole said: Who are you? What are you doing?
Nothing was moving yet to its end.

No perfumes: it needs the warmth of day. Almost the first fire in the northeast, a pink powder, scattered.

AUGUST

Even in brightest daylight the day averts its face,
So what can frighten it or make it ashamed?

*

1961

MARCH

Heart more dark than the violet
(eye soon closed again by the chasm)
learn to exhale that fragrance
which opens so gentle a way
across the impassable.

1962

MARCH

"Since he's not a god I show him the way. Not in the forest (the leaves are too treacherous), not even in the night (what could be more tender for him, more luminous than the night, more wonderful than those mirrors, those flames, that dark colour) I tell him to go beyond, I don't even tell him to go but to destroy, not even to look but to close his eyes as the diver does when fear comes over him.

"Go neither up nor down, just destroy, only seek what is not difficult, only seek what cannot be kept, what is impossible: last chance, and not promised, not even certain, or just probable. Let him just go on his way again; let him not stand there like a beggar, a thief, a weakling I'm ashamed of (but I don't tell)."

*

Start from nothing. That is my law. All the rest: smoke, far off.

*

Beauty: scattered like a seed, left to the winds, the storms, without a sound, often lost, always destroyed; but it persists, blossoms haphazardly, now here, now there, fed by shadows, the funereal earth, welcomed by the depth. Light, brittle, almost invisible, apparently without force, exposed, abandoned, surrendered, obedient—it ties itself to what is heavy, immobile—and a flower opens on a mountain slope. It is. It persists in the teeth of noise, folly; tenacious among blood and malediction, in the life you cannot take upon yourself, live; so does the spirit go round in spite of everything, and of necessity ridiculous, unpaid, unconvincing. So, too, must you go on, scatter, risk words, give them exactly the weight you want, never stop until the end—against, always against yourself and the world, before you can finally go beyond the opposition, with words, precisely, words that cross the border line, the wall, words that

25

make their way, overcome, open, and finally triumph, sometimes, in perfume, in colour—one instant, only one instant.
That, at least, is what I cling to, to say what is almost nothing,
or to say only that I am going to say it, which is still a positive
action, better than inaction or the action of withdrawal, re-
fusal, denial. Fire, the cock, dawn: Saint Peter. That I remember. At the end of the night, when the fire still burns in the
room and day breaks outside and the cock crows, like the very
song of the fire that tears itself loose from the night. "And he
wept bitterly." Fire and tears, dawn and tears.

For the hundredth time: I am left with almost nothing.
but it's like a very small door you have to pass through, and
nothing proves that the space beyond will not be as vast as
you imagined. All that matters is to pass through the door, and
that it should not fall shut for ever.

*

Let silent grief at least
Hatch out that last chance
Of light.

Let that extremity of wretchedness
Preserve the chance of flowers.

*

It is as if you could not, would no longer speak. You must pass
through there if you will not cheat, not lie.

APRIL

Monument to the impossible. The best of yourself given,
in total loss, to what will never be obtained.

Flowers of the peach tree given to the bees of fire.

No more turning away: go back like a whip to its mark.
Looks, words like whips.

26

From the coals of the night, on the black branches of the night, that blossoming, that pink grace, and soon after the humming bees of the day.

Let whoever wants to, recognize what is most beautiful in the world in this heraldic scene—what man discovers when insomnia wakes him at the end of the night—and what lifts him up later, like a wing, above himself.

MAY

Rain on thousands of leaves and what burns deep down in man. Fire, twisting.

Eight o'clock. At night. Above the chestnut trees laden with flowers, above those perfumes, those emanations, that agitation, that activity, the surprising blue of heaven, luminous and dark at the same time, profoundly blue, much bluer than during the day, and the clouds with their blinding domes.

Also that water running in the earth, right in the sun: memory of a mountain stream. Water, and its facets, its blades or scales of sun. Its clues. Burying its mirrors.

SEPTEMBER/IBIZA

Strong wind, froth on the waves, brilliant against a dark background. Thunderstorms to the left, sun on the right, Tintoretto? A theatre in the sky, changing all the time.

Stand aside, reappear: the games of light. You wake up from a long torpor. Folds of the sea and more folds, small snowy mountains, soon vanished or pushed up again elsewhere, in no apparent order. Here, then there. Cold moss, dark. Short blossoming out against the rocks. Falling, crashes, sound of masses of water breaking, collapsing.

The essence of a small island, agitation, instability?

Places of wind with bushes resting on the earth, roots also, as if lying in a herbarium of pink soil. Seaweed almost silvered when dry.

*

Fires, invisible, burning most intense; they exist somehow, like what is between things and does not appear, except when the things it links change or grow.

Souls live like that, maybe, like those fires, working in secret like them.

Those fires, those chains. Such are the distances between one tree and the next, one boat and the next. A first star appears, because the light grows softer, as when a veil is lifted. The sky, its colour, seems to grow denser, grow velvet with pink, grey, purplish blue. The star seems to shine in an immense cloud of smoke, a perfume.

Skies dark as ashes. The thought of ashes above the pine trees that shake their branches, their crests almost yellow, luminous against that threatening background.

Their answer to the monotonous, pigheaded wind: full of grace, and trembling, somewhat, but rather calm, patient, anyway, discreet, elegant. A continuous quivering without weariness, the art of almost not yielding, of turning weakness into charm. More complex in the olive tree, more clumsy in the carob tree. All these words just above the ground, animated by an invisible threat, repaying terror with beauty.

OCTOBER

Light like dust: autumn
Or on the contrary a mirror.

*

As if you entered into another melody, a sweet song: it calls you back—sirens—suggests, advises, at a time when there seem to be only reefs in front.

*

Flowers bloom with another colour in autumn, a special colour, while their leaves grow lighter and change. Old colours, grown old—like rust, fire dying. Season of mushrooms, their smell, products of the rain. They look like sponges, molluscs (slugs that venture out after the rain), very crumbly, colourless in most cases, or else with the colour of rats, earth, wood. Plants hidden, as if on the sly, half buried under bundles of wet leaves, lightish plants, with a white, fragile stem (what is white, what lives in the earth: larvae, link between ghosts and mushrooms, but fog, also) with those hats, those wheels with tiny partitions, like the pages of a concentric book, like ship's screws . . . but one shouldn't overdo the descriptive bits. You want to walk in the woods. Night, with the moon, all is still smoke, wet and cold suspense. The traveler in the car, who passes through this world as if riding in a dream—either his torments grow less violent, if he has any, or else his happiness grows in that illusion of lightness, if he is happy. A secret appears in those hills without losing its secret character.

Hölderlin: *Hier in dieser Unschuld des Lebens, hier unter den silbernen Alpen* . . . Letter written from Hauptwyl. For me the essence of the poet shows in the beginning of that sentence, which has the purity of some rare passages from the *Saison en Enfer: Quelquefois je vois au ciel* . . . It is the whiteness of the mushrooms in reverse. Angels and larvae, angels and ghosts. But white all the same.

Colours: born from evil? Whiteness which is absence of colours, or death; whiteness which is essence of colours, or life transcended, maybe.

*

That smoke for a moment in the light, that memory of fire, that farewell which is an instant above the earth, still, the room, all I know—and I can scarcely go forward any more. The feather that points to a flight, a nest.

The forest must have burnt, there are only these feathers left, they will change into rain.

Wool, perfume.

*

Those last pink petals, colour of exquisite shame, of secret fire, those confessions of the earth. While the garden burns itself out without flame, grows yellow, brown, dries up. Stems break. The hidden earth will reappear. It isn't gold on the trees, the vine, rather the colour of a very clear flame—and it also gives an impression of rest, not warmth. Yellow . . . What mingled with the grass and other plants in the past begins to look different, changes and shows itself, only to bring the end closer. Shows itself and shows how brittle it has grown, emaciated, admits to wear and tear, fraying out, being torn, soiled. How difficult to grasp what is essential! One is always tempted to go too far or not far enough, to be too vague or too precise. These things should be grasped suddenly, but exactly, like a shot from a rifle. There are, indeed, hunters in those yellow vineyards—gunsmoke, birds fly up, suddenly, dogs bark—a threat of mist, a kernel of cold in the sunny air. The birds are threatened when the leaves grow lighter. Autumn has colours of feathers, furs, foxes, dogs. Autumn looks less like plants; trees put on their masks, their disguises. Fatal feast, deadly in a way. The trees are like cocks—in the air that grows cold, in the sun that grows pale. They also look like the sun in October, pale yellow at first, then dark red when it enters into the haze on the horizon. Pheasant colours. And the clouds enjoy being pink above these aviaries, these farmyards. The mind savours these days when forests grow lighter, are pierced, when a softness persists in the air around a kernel of cold. It suddenly sees, at dawn, a bunch of trees in the mist, like gems in a nest of flock, like a sun of leaves in the clouds. Like a jewel in linen.

*

One can no longer make out things clearly.

One is thrust back on incomprehension.

The last thoughts are jostled.
The world is reduced to the stirring of the morning wind.

*

New world
no longer of thoughts
nor yet of axioms to develop peacefully until death
but a pavillion of pictures
Protected from space not by a wall
but by visions

No question now of living on firm land
one is carried away
One possesses nothing now but the fleeting
All that is sure goes out like a snuffed lamp.
One hurls oneself on to a source that has fled
One is nourished by the morning wind.

DECEMBER

Again, before the day, that rest, that blue, that divine eye.
And the earth frozen as if withdrawn, shut off, like wood
hollowed out by worms.

Then the scattering of gold dust, fog, the hills like boats
in the fog.

A flight of pigeons over a farm, far.

*

Lamp switched off—grave of rain.

Lamp suddenly switched off. What its light was like, in the
night, when the others burn no more.

*

The pink at night on or in the mountains, that fire. Eyes
almost, a glow. Under the sky, blue without end.

*

Night, and before it flees, its fringes, its moiré of fire.

*

Before the day, in Winter, between the mountains and the dark clouds, on the black silhouette of the trees like a pole, flags in rags, pale pink or purple (and they will be pink in the evening), announcing the army of light.

1963

JANUARY

I had a mirror
In which it was no longer me that I saw
But eyelids closed over embers
A world pink and profound

I must break it
Before it hides the air from me

*

Oh, that fire which runs anew to the dawn
Born of the horizon's sleep
And on the panes that spittle of frost
The fire that blazes up because the mountains have
     lain down
Because they have closed their eyes

In the blue of sleep a fire begins
Mountains dreaming
Lovers

*

Flowers.
They prepare themselves among dry bones, in the mansion under the earth, among the dead, or also in the land of dreams,

in a dense mass with fire at its centre. The earth itself, a fruit, with a kernel of fire; suspended under its foliage of clouds.

Ice, waves, leaves of frost. You can still see those things, but you don't see them as things any more but as emanations, ideas, shapes, movements, births.

Sometimes the whole world like a light bubble, like a whirl of snow our eyes alone think motionless or weighty.

*

I'll spend the night in this boat. No lantern fore or aft. Nothing but a few stars in the water, mother of pearl, and the sleepy movement of the current. I shall land on a dubious shore, marked out by the rare cries of the first birds, frightened.

Souls taken from this world, why not hope for a similar landing place? There may well be some kinds of cries, unknown, a look that nothing stops, not to be exhausted—something that goes beyond all understanding, all imagination, all desire?

*

Black cascade suspended
Mysterious thing, horselike
Plumage
A thing to twist
Burning close to our centre
Fleece, brand, inverted torch
Flame of night by day
Iron in our hearts

MARCH

First buds, first leaves
Evenings that grow larger and lighter
Violets, why
So dark, so fragrant?

MAY

The light has been taken out of the trees' lamp

*

All has been pushed back into another world
Frontier
I shall not pass it again
Someone is walking on the other side
Or was I dreaming?

All night I follow that footfall
By day, I can hardly advance

JUNE

In the flowering lime tree
beyond its tumescence
its hum
the sight
of the evening sky
the passage of light

Only that awakens me now
that far-off sleep

Nothing but luminous air
and somewhere the fire that sleeps.
Only that now, on this day
the immense world
the house of birds
and the nest of sleep

34

SEPTEMBER

The trees and the gardens caught in a washhouse haze at night, but cold, and stars above. Then fine weather in the morning, out of that nest of fog.

*

Poplars, tutors of smoke, against the light, waiting for the day.

1964

JANUARY

Winter so rightly named, with the quick bird's name
Season clear and bare
Taking a straighter way than any other
Season bent like a bow
Time of the birds brought near
Of the high aerial reeds
Mother of pearl and earth
Glass and straw

*

Shadow from nowhere, anywhere, corrupts or tears apart. Things torn off the world, wounds of the world.

A cart slowly on the road, carrying dead things, a fragment of time—which remains, in rags, in the memory, sweet and cruel, until memory too is carried away, commemoration forgotten.

*

The hamlet of Teyssières, towards the source of the Lez, with the clear water. On the east side of the Lance, steep, dark now, pine trees mingle with others like fans, dark pink. A river runs under the ice at the bottom of a comb. The earth is humid, heavy, cold. Box trees and mulberry bushes grow along the road. The hamlet, shivering in the shadows of snow, like a lost pig farm, with only old men left. You can see their faces, stupid or haggard behind the windows, against a background of soot.

*

Like a saw cutting through wood
Destruction rips the heart
Time in the thickness of the air

*

To have to watch the night, the suffering it shelters, instead of sleep.

You can only deal with the impossible, then, set the possible against the impossible. There is an extreme moment when that becomes necessary (I am not talking about myself, only about what I have guessed and what is common to all of us). At that limit only mute prayer can begin again, the soul shrivelled in fear and spite, the mind unarmed. Only a senseless murmur can begin again, as if without a place, direction, space, stammering in the depths. Maybe without a purpose too, existing only in itself, lost. Against the teeth of the saw that rends. At that point, when action is absolutely powerless, when the hand can only stop, fall back, impotent.

*

You hear sighs: as of somebody who carries too heavy a burden of pleasure or of pain. Labour. Like somebody possessed by the violence of the night. You have been struck down, you still are, but by an opposite power, as fulness is set against the void, fire against ice. Who has ill-treated you like that? You were a perfumed fire, now you are broken and trembling, you will be thrown away with the rubbish, hidden in the earth. Your beauty troubled the mind; it cannot bear the horror of your end, not even in thought, from afar.

*

Monteverdi: the flame that changes into ornament without ceasing to burn. More than any other music it gives an impres-

sion of fire, night and stars. It bears on both Shakespeare and
Titian (The Vienna *Danae*, for instance). But rather than a
golden rain descending on her nudity, it seems, in these melo-
dies, as if body, substance, coloured, velvety density, a trans-
forming power rises to the highest peaks of heaven, a power
you could almost *grasp* in certain arabesques like the one
adorning the word *stelle* in *Ed è pur dunque vero* or the word
prezzo in the *Lettera amorosa* (the text of which precisely
plays on hair that is at the same time a flame and a golden
rain.) These figures, like flowers opening, always remain linked
to the subterranean world of passion. Nothing, also, could be
more in harmony with Tasso's text in the *Fight of Tancredo
and Crolinda*, so voluptuous in spite of its moralizing ending.

*

Speaking costs the lips so little
But fixing them to the wound
If that is the only way
I shall have rotted unable to pass
Through this putrid needle's eye.

JUNE

Now everything is less easy
Gentleness almost forgotten
One is more prudent with words
Now the flight falls back
The wing limps
There is weight on the back of my neck
And I hardly dream any more
Or differently
Now I feel the need to be slashed

*

Broch's gloss on the "Letter of Lord Chandos" neglects an
important element. Something subsists at the height of the

crisis: "A watering pot, a harrow left out in the fields . . . can become the vessels of my liberation." This sheds light on modern poetry. "Rather a shepherd's fire than the majestic tones of the organ. . . ." Harmony, complete and durable, is broken; we are left with fragments and, between them, an almost unliveable void that threatens to engulf them.

JULY

Farm. Under the big oaks: harrow, grindstone, well, blue wheelbarrow, hoops of a barrel. Shadow and wind. Farther away, poplars in a circle of shadow at their feet (noon) before wheat and lavender.

*

A prisoner, only now one lives, not while one is detached.
In these sweating chains, smooth, gentle
Wanting this chaining up, this blinding
In this dark and brilliant water, in this cage of sighs
Bath
As though inside a fruit

*

Fig: fire in a wrapping of night, or else a kind of sponge,
        of spongy coral always on the point of decay.
Wood wasps frantically coupled.

*

OCTOBER

Violent wind: yellow leaves suddenly fly up. Black, rapid clouds, eclipsing the sun for a moment. Always white birds, doves in the distance. Their colour, in the bed of the wind, the bed of time, while you grow older, while you worry, or while you are afraid of catastrophes you cannot even bear to think of. No truth beyond this?

Children, as helpless as those leaves.

NOVEMBER

Seven in the morning: chestnut trees like a flame in the fog; the green of the grass between the roots of the vine, intense and clear. Difficult to grasp what evokes the strangeness of those trees (where birds still cry). Aggressive car engines. A hunter, bent and skinny, passes quickly, engraved by Callot.

1965

JANUARY

A walk in the clear, soft weather. A spot where the river has left vast expanses of pebbles and mud, with dead wood, from previous floods. A dyke protects the fields. You can see the snow on the Ventoux, on the hills. Three poplars planted in the shelter of the dyke's embankment, a meadow, and rows of cypresses beyond, protecting the tilled land. A thicket of high trembling poplars farther away, and sawed-off trunks at their feet, big white stones in the round: once again the place of an almost sacred combination—mysterious at least and touching—or natural elements under a pure and brittle light. In the cage of the trees, in their web, under their sparse magic. Arms of water that are not dead, a shiver brings their surface to life and the water is clear, too (no weeds, nothing crawls). The wings of winter.

AUGUST

The fig tree moving under the moon at night. It would seem that you need only wait, in a night as calm as this one, to hear the wind rising, weak like the sound of breathing, rumpling the leaves of the fig tree and the vine (they produce a sound both sweet and abrupt, harsh, as of paper). Then you see the fig tree, all black, moving slowly, serenely, the world seems to be enclosed in it for a moment, because of that light movement in the middle of a vast silence. Because there is an unusual silence, not one car passing by, not one dog barking. It seems that you begin to see again, a tree seems utterly incomprehensible, once more.

*

SEPTEMBER

The impossible events, what you have to read or see in the papers every day, unbearable, to say all. It seems impossible to go on, therefore, and yet you do. Why?

Because poetry could be of some help in confronting the unbearable. Confront is a big word.

What makes it difficult for me to express myself is that I would like not to cheat—and it seems to me that most people cheat, more or less, on their own experience, put it between brackets, whisk it away. From then on a number of words should enter into poetry, a number of words it has always avoided, been afraid of—but still without moving towards naturalism, which is just as much of a lie, in its own way.

There is a range between Beckett and Saint-John Perse, who are the two extremes, and both systematically so.

But it means being a hair's breadth away from the impossible—always.

*

You children who are inventive, how you will be slapped!

*

No word seems to be weighty enough, or simple enough, to hold its own beside the unnameable; that is what one is looking for.

Plough. The plough that cuts man off from sweetness, light. Who leans on its handle, its share?

So little time. Such short notice. How can you grasp anything at all? You have hardly finished your dream when other dreamers push you out of the way.

*

Maybe we should try for a diction that is less metaphysical: death becomes care, then, patience, fear, weakness, wounds and bandages, no big words, not even a struggle, but only gestures, smiles, tears, wakes. No revelation: patience, pain, anguish, wonder. Weakness above all, maybe, the weakness of a child, a child in distress. Nothing grandiose. And yet . . .

*

The voice of a child: all on a high and gracious register, conjures up words like cattle bells; and behind them the freshness of grass, meadows in the mountains, where you hear them mostly at night, which is blue.

*

Apple trees in the orchard. That purple red, that yellow of wax; grasp their meaning. Low trees, laden, close, linked together. Shadow and the grass under it. Autumn. The river in which the branches of the walnut tree dip their ends, or almost.

To speak about embers, globes of embers as I did in a poem in *Airs* is an unsatisfactory approximation, partly false. The word "purple" gets one thing right, not everything. There is the roundness, the hardness of the pulp; but you shouldn't take the magnifying glass to everything. Just that it should be grasped *in passing* and *from afar, deeply and immediately.* I am, in the final analysis, not so much concerned with the *tree's specific qualities*, something Ponge applies himself to,

41

superbly well. One grasps a combination of elements in the wink of an eye; but it is not at all abstract or general either, because other essences will have an analogous, if not identical effect. There is the impression of fire, a fire as if asleep in a nest of leaves; there is the impression of a ball, roundness, a sphere, that of a fruit in general; but, characteristic for the apple tree, maybe some rudeness, peasant rusticity, something rough rather than harmonious, irregular in any case, rude, simple, common. The opposite of the exotism or the luxury other fruit trees here could conjure up, and nothing Biblical, like the fig tree. It is the countryside of Europe, therefore childhood too, parents, home. Something central. *Domestic* trees. Maids. Maids on the farm. You should bring together what is near and what is far away, what is permanent and what is momentary, in the same way, what is common and what is not—and in one single moment, fresh and as if free of care, not through application, perseverance, labour, etc. All search should vanish. In passing, while the mind is busy with other things, maybe even in despair, that sign has been given, that gift.

*

Persistent uneasiness, fear with a better word, about the future. And yet another autumn opens like a cradle, you are as if suspended in light, white, motionless and warm, among the raisins that grow heavier and darker, the figs that ferment, full of flies and wasps. How do you untie yourself?

*

Another day of that blinding suspense. Trembling carcass on this sweet and luminous space.

Blue lavender flowers with a yellow heart, blue violet, purple rose, in falling bunches.

Big yellow flowers among the shades of dark green, their intensity—"suns" would be a bad translation, once again. Undecipherable yellow, and yet it should be deciphered, as if to be reinforced.

Children set free in sleep.

1966

MARCH

The little pink peach tree, in the distance, on a spot of light green meadow. Nothing else, an arrow that hollows out our deepest depths.

*

MAY

A field of sainfoin, not really pink, but almost the colour of the earth, the colour of charcoal almost burnt up. Nightingales in all the bushes.

Crown of white roses. The big rose bush reminded me of the sparse, unkempt hair of an old man who is gravely ill, this year. And now also of Lear in the storm. He has no strength left; the slightest smell is torture, and yet he was the least squeamish of men.

*

Perfume of flowers: to smell an iris or a rose is the only gesture that takes me back to childhood, immediately, irresistibly; and not as if I remembered one of its moments, but as if I was taken there, for as long as a flash of lightning. Strange that the presence of a time already far off could have grafted itself onto what is most brittle, most invisible, the breath of creatures so ephemeral.

*

I understand the movement of the mountains better; slow ascension and concentration at the same time. And, moreover, if I say "mountain," now, there is the thing and, underneath, felt or not, the idea, whereas the word "ascension" deprives the idea of its life, therefore of the fulness of its truth, by making it more abstract. That is, maybe, the weakness of the type of painting called abstract; to have wanted to bring to the fore what was hidden, modestly, at times even unconsciously, in other styles.

You will say that it is no longer possible to pretend to be innocent in this day and age; that one should work (paint, write) *with* all the knowledge stored up in one's consciousness. But some ignorance remains, whatever you do, and fairly constant. (Ungaretti in what he wrote for Michaux)

*

A walk in the long evening. High grass under the leafy trees. The stones, so old. Wells and springs like old tombs—or altars—sometimes in the shadow of an almond tree; and also old tombs and monuments like fountains.

*

Link between soul and ugliness. The love-making of plants, insects. It doesn't look shameful (from outside) until you get to the higher animals. The same is true of wounds, illness etc. When we go towards things, therefore, we do it because of a dream of innocence, as for a baptism.

What place do you set aside for the ignoble? The price of a higher mode of being. What do you reach through your wounds? Wound of the eyes.

Rebaptised every morning by the light of day.

Bunches of honeysuckle. I live in a Greek country.

*

There is that shadow of pain behind me now, whatever I write, it makes all the poems I have written seem too fluid, and almost every sentence as well, because no word is pain, on the contrary, it is detached, intact.

A wounded light, as I imagine it in front of the Cologne Rembrandt, is that not Christ? We could no longer believe in a godhead that could be intact; that was no longer enough. But a god whose wounds alone are visible? So my turn has come, too, to discover myself between the young Greek gods and the crucified god, between the gods of youth and the gods that had to appear when mankind felt old and ill. I have

44

changed much less than I happened to think, I am back at old Mme G's bedside, with a candle, in the big room with the shutters closed. I keep repeating the same thing; if only it could grow closer and closer to the truth.

*

Whatever links us to the elementary and the very old in the landscapes of the present, is a witness to their greatness, compared to other landscapes where those images (sometimes no more than illusions, but significant) are not present, or present to a lesser degree. The worn stone especially, stained with lichens, close to furs or plants; bark; walls that have become useless in the woods; wells; houses invaded by ivy and abandoned. At this moment in history, when man is farther removed than ever from the elementary, landscapes in which man-made monuments are hard to distinguish from rocks and from the earth disturb us to the depths of our being, keep the dream of a kind of return to the origins alive—a dream that appeals to many people who are frightened by the strange future that is emerging. We see that there is no big difference between the Alyscamps and the abandoned quarries at Saint Restitut that bring the Forum to mind. We feel that those wells and underground canalizations, dug by the Romans, maybe, or maybe much later, and it doesn't matter, put us in touch with a pagan mystery. Is it only a game? Or an escape? We seem to find columns scattered everywhere, traces of temples. What does it mean, what does it give us, what does it teach us? We discover certain *places*, we often walk across them, and yet we can't seem to find them at will. What is a *place*? A kind of centre brought into relation with a whole. No longer an isolated spot, lost, futile. On this bridge people used to build altars, erect stones. High and low communicate in places, and because a place is a centre you do not feel the need to leave it; rest reigns there, meditation. Our church could well be that enclosure with dismantled walls where oaks grow in silence, where a rabbit runs across, from time to time, or a partridge. We hesitate to enter the others because of the intellectual schemata they put between ourselves and the divine.

That, of course, does not solve anything. I think we might still have accepted the risk of venturing out and going under, in a world woven only of such places. Places help us; those who go looking for them, often without even knowing why, are not growing in number for nothing. They can't stand to be strangers in space any longer. They start breathing again, they believe life is possible again only in places. We have, in a way, benefited from their gifts and we have made ourselves an existence less false than many others. But that includes a strange aloofness from all preoccupations of the moment, and more than one danger. Anyway, let us recognize our privileges.

Culture and innocence: the best in culture always keeps a reflection of the original innocence; it is not its opposite. The works we love are also in contact with "places," even if they are of a different kind, etc. The only culture is what preserves and passes on innocence, what is native. The rest should be given another name.

The good hatches in our silence; in our isolation ripens the power to break it.

*

We are accompanied by bending shadows
The farther one goes the more the tool digs into the skin
We are filled with ineffectual pity
A tree of sadness grows deep inside us
Nothing is harder than not to forestall one's death
When it seems that there is nothing left to wait for
Save more decrepitude still and more pain

*

Yet one is still in the coolness, the light
The capacity for a little goodness is not lost
One can still change life at any moment
With much attention and gentleness.
(Perpetual bendingness of the course of things
At least as long as there is time for it.
Later it is others who will hold out.)

*

At the limit of his weariness
What does he bear?
He crashes down on to his shadow,
Saturated with pity.
Putrescence attacks his words
He can no longer keep it out of his heart
Now there is no place
Words are like routed soldiers
What power could reorder them?
No magic helps any more.
Endless or distant torments grow like mountains.

*

For a long time I kept away wounds
With the passing of birds
I was surrounded by air and feathers
At present my skin is still intact
But they have entered into me
Sometimes they bleed, especially at night
I still see the birds
But I bleed as they fly
When I merely hear them
Without seeing them, at the heart of day
I feel a little spared.

JUNE

The long evenings, warmer, the moon pink or orange, the world blue, suspended, full of sweetness.

Full of horror.

*

Full of sweetness, really, and as if of kindness. Those nights of full moon, yellow rather than pink or orange, when the trees seem to breathe because of the weak wind, are like a balm. They unknot the heart, calm and tepid. Slow, imperceptible ascension of that wheat-coloured globe; breath of leaves; crickets and owls, nightingales, the only sounds that last. Let us bathe in that milky water, if only for a moment, before we are put on the rack. Let us speak or sleep in that cradle of air.

*

The emotional connotation of words: the more hidden, the greater, probably. What Chagall told me about Mozart: the more his music is transparent, the more you can feel death in it. I am not sure if that is right, but there is a truth and a beauty in that thought. Rule of contradiction: the more literature wants to be pure inspiration, the more it seems verbal (surrealism). Which does not mean, of course, that it should be verbal to seem inspired.

*

To keep things in their rightful place and not let death encroach on life in vain. Necessity, blessing of limitations, (re-reading Henri Michaux, with unbroken admiration).

Let limitations be like the old walls of these forests, these fields: old, human, evoking less a stop, a closure, than a kind of justice and a putting in order, too, without pedantry, fertile. *Mysterious barricades.* Fruitful measure.

*

This year when the crown of white roses
Made me think of hair ruffled and greying
On the brow of an old man who suffers and accepts with
    a sad courage
And also of the old king of the storm
Men so worthy by virtue of their age and their humble
    knowledge
Beside whom youth seems stupid and boisterous . . .
If we could have some of that wisdom and that courage
Rather than too much vain knowledge and dreams.
We lose them and still they go with us.
The light lasts longer than the lamp

48

So that the concatenation of clarities shall not be broken.
Now that I have seen death it fascinates me almost less than
　　　when it was unknown
I feel like turning away from it as from a thing incomplete
　　　and perhaps meaningless.
It seems to me that today's light has grown
Like a plant.

*

I want nothing now but to remove
that which divides us from brightness
only to give room
to the heart's fruit ripening

I hear old men
who are in tune with day
I learn patience at their feet.

*

Goodness pierces through, lets in air. Cruelty locks up. Link
between theatre and eroticism: red, black and gold. Sade's
castles.

*

The child says it thinks of sad things at night, the death
of its parents. Like quick birds in its sky; their shadow on its
eyes, its source.

JULY

If today I listen to the sound of the days
what shall I hear
only the falling of days
into the unknown deep?
One is made of gleams, one has no more existence
than a knot of water and of gleams

Life gradually turned into images, reduced to images
that are filtered inside us.
The poet transmits the purest of them.
Our body of images, of memory.

AUGUST

Heat that nourishes, sets on fire, disheartens. The world
seems lost indeed, at times; a total view of it is impossible
to bear, a view that encompasses its violence, its shame. Children exposed like that, clear eyes, joy in their heart.

*

All I have written, and, particularly, the clearest, the most
serene lines, I have, without a doubt, written only to push
back the unknown, to keep it at a distance, the fear that is
coming closer now, and triumphs, sometimes, at night.

The brush of mortal light that is supposed to open up
the future for us drives us out of hiding everywhere.

Where is the Being that will give us strength? Who will
give us a moment of respite when we can almost no longer
break out of weariness? What is the resurrection? The story
of a dream?

That Being is farther away than the farthest point in the
sky, more unknown than the unknown. A child has ample time
to scream before it intervenes.

How do you build?

There are times when I understand those wretched young
people who sleep on the stones of our towns and are only
vaguely aroused by desire, from time to time: why walk upright, why procreate, why maintain in such a world? Their
laziness no doubt responds all too eagerly to that resignation.

Others are always in a hurry. Girls just old enough to get
married bare their legs and, fed on attractive pictures, look for
whoever will snatch them from their floating boredom by
means of the pleasure they have come to expect. You can see

it even in the streets of the village; each of them has her little machine that follows her around (like the hunter his dog, the buffoon his king), blaring out the innuendoes of the new witches in the supermarkets, potions made of the rubbish in dustbins spill out of it, without interruption. They walk, swaying their hips, smoking, vaguely drunk on that musty taste of radio-exhaust, so pretty often with the fresh colours of their dresses, their cunning hair styles, so animal on their long brown legs, so stupid—or in such distress that they see themselves as flagships cruising off "splendid cities."

They are in a hurry; they paint their faces in a hurry, like savages for their war, they go out, they close their eyes, they want to enjoy themselves, they will soon be old, or else everything will be pestilential ash. But whatever they do, if only they knew how quickly their colours will fade, how their paint and their feathers will soon bathe in tears. They run, straining against the bridle, around the hive of engines, in the noise of concrete mixers, in front of houses built to crumble quickly. The patience they will need to pay for that race! But who could blame them, knowing the world in which they live. Like an anthill, and an enormous stick has poked into it, one day, to see. The stick of Hiroshima. The cudgel of knowledge.

They run, they think they are launching themselves on their course and all they do is run away. Don't expect them to make any kind of effort; their skull already rejects all non-premasticated food; it has to run in their ears like a very fluid balm, and it must run without interruption. Interruption is an effort in itself, a risk. They embalm themselves with insipid molasses, sugar will soon seem too bitter for their taste. Or else, when they get out of their lethargy, they want to be shocked, shaken; they were larvae, nymphs of insects, they have become puppets. They are shaken, beaten. They open their mouths, will there be foam on their lips? Then they cave in under the pressure of sound. Nymphs of Castalia, dryads . . . Dismantled insects, nothing more. Blinded by the new sun, the sun of hell; knocked down by its cudgel.

NOVEMBER

The first snow: how the flakes melt when they come closer to the earth, the roofs; disappear. I think of the kiss that comes closer to the body, to the skin. Also of what changes and seems to disappear. Like the death of a bird, a butterfly. A dissipation.

*

In the friendship of the forests. Why do stones, tender moss, ivy, dead wood, mushrooms, all that makes up the soil of the undergrowth seem to be so *good* to us? As if we were carried in a hand, welcomed and supported. Bed and table in one?

Water trickling down on the rocks: as if they split open.

Under the trees, under the perforated screen of the oaks: more than that. Absurd as it may seem, the word "friendship" is on my tongue again. With their blessing. Their light, their trembling mediation, their serenity between our heart and the infinite that is too heavy. Their roof, porous, moves in the slightest wind. Leaf: between bird and tile. Under those thousands of winged or floating tiles, under that filter of light, of the infinite. Under those fans winter strips to a rugged broomstick.

And so you yield to the motions of the mind that looks for analogies, you let yourself be carried away to another kind of pleasure or beauty; and once again you have to say "that wasn't it," when it's over. It was the earth, the wood, the greenery, the sky; a walk, a moment's respite, a bit more innocence. It was also what seems eternal because it always starts again, the same and without monotony. It was Time when he smiles like a patriarch, when she smiles like a mother. The immemorial. What sets itself against the stultified mind. The open house. The forest is a house with doors and windows open. Light moves through it as on the streets. Passes, leaves and enters. Light, or your dream, naked, never to be caught again?

*

And suddenly you see yellow trees under the ever moving clouds. But that doesn't mean you can actually show that yellow, which is neither that of a lemon, nor that of wheat, nor that of the sun. There is something pale about it, something cold. The colour of certain feathers (and the whole landscape like an aviary full of canaries?).

(A leaf, closeup: you see that the yellow is the green grown pale, discoloured, and the green itself is still there, where the leaf was joined to the stem. The green withdraws, flees like water, and the undertone of yellow invades the surface.)

The water glitters in the muddy furrows, or looks like bits of iron.

Those leaves are really fires elsewhere. The idea of a change is very present; of an attack, a wound, and a reaction to that attack. Colours of the setting sun (noticed before, but very true). Answer to Time? All forests like setting suns, as if the year's sun was setting.

Also: the last screens, last decorations. Before you see the frame. The earth is a shell with scales. Leave us alone with the rain under the rafters of heaven. Leave us naked, but stronger.

*

. . . As in the hour before the day, a man walking, vaguely, crossing the road, he seems without strength, lost; nothing to help him, to support him.

*

Everyday things: light the fire (and it doesn't catch on the first time, because the wood is not dry, because you should have piled it up outside, and that takes time), think of the children's homework, a bill unpaid, a sick acquaintance to visit, etc. How does poetry insert itself into all this? Either it is just an ornament, or else it should be inside all those gestures, or acts: that is how Simone Weil understood religion, how Michel Deguy understands poetry, how I want it understood. There is still the danger of artifice, or a "diligent," laborious sacralization. It might relegate us to a more modest position, intermediary: poetry lights up life from time to time like snow, falling, and you have achieved a great deal already if you have kept eyes to see it. Maybe one should agree to let it keep its *exceptional* nature, which is so characteristic. Do what you can between the two, by hook or by crook. You might run the risk of sectarian seriousness otherwise, the temptation to wear the poet's mantle, to cut yourself off in "prayer" (which is a bit embarrassing in Rilke, at times). I have to accept more weakness, for myself at least.

*

Seven-thirty in the morning. The air, motionless. The whole earth is blue, the whole earth is sleep. The rare clouds that are still grey grow pink while you write them down. Just that slight red, that inflammation on the edge of the mountains.

1967

FEBRUARY

All the trees, in the evening, a pink armful, ready for the fire.

Their branches, still naked, glisten with heavenly water in the morning. They spread light. Luminous bushels?

*

Rain, birds cry, the first flowers of the almond tree: their harmony makes you happy. Maybe it is as when you hear the same thing in the different voices of a choir? Or as when you see a multitude of flowers born from a single trunk? Thousands, thousands of cries, a thousand flowers, a thousand globes of sonorous water, and one single world, one single hearth?

MARCH

Almond trees, from a distance: foam over the landscape, against the dark background of ashes, earth.

54

Closeup: green, white, yellow, that harmony so short that one hardly has the time to grasp it. Colour of milk.

MAY

The earth in cracks, in scales, like a ruin. Fertile, flowery ruins. Everything builds up from a central spot, and widens, multiplies, or scatters itself. Genealogical trees. Doomed, bold seeds. To feel yourself a seed of a very old plant—you can't see the roots any more.

*

Mountain on its base, lifted by light. Fruit in a glass of light. Buddhas are sometimes carried like that. They cannot be shaken, toppled.

I remember the bridge, that cold day in March, the black arch of the bridge of Rust, in Burgenland, the strong impression it made on me. Day of birds and mother of pearl, and those long boats, and those crossings towards the lake, between the reeds.

Straw partitions: shelter and lightness. The right measure, the right distance from the enclosure. The copse of the Côte d'Or, its hedges and its sleepy rivers, meandering.

The harrow of the reeds.

*

It is still in the realms of magic for me, the low mountain under the almost white sky, beyond a close field, beyond the trees against the light, humming with wind; the mountain as a patch of sky, less clear. What is it, then?

A dome as seen from here, a flattened ridge and the sky is even more light above it.

No volume, no relief, no details, rising above the trees, and more light too, where it touches their tops; hence the impression that it is light, floating, suspended. Colour? Hardly: like smoke in the air.

I had guessed an essential element of that magic before:

lightness. I think I am discovering another one this morning. Hard to define. It struck me as I turned around. It was (I think) as if there had been some presence (friendly) on my left, somebody (protection?). Maybe tied up with childhood memories?

As if I had always had that blue presence on my left, as far back as my memory goes, by no means heavy or hostile, on the contrary: benevolent.

I think it must be, once again, for me, another image of the happy *limit* that does not stifle.

Mountain—house.

*

JULY

Hollyhocks, carried into the crystalline evening after the sun has set, fascinating. You are tempted to think of the word incarnate, carnation, therefore of flesh, turning pink. But I think the connection is very vague, almost as in a dream, it must be something else. And yet it is not impossible that that flower represents the dream of a pure and burning sexuality, relieved of the weight of humours, moods. Without a blot, but real. Maybe all things are just that, deep down.

Openings, carried at the top of a pole, in the crystal of the night.

Silent megaphones. Vases full of pollen. Almost transparent. As if the plant changed itself into sky, or into wings, at least. The *pink* plays an essential part. Pink flowers, flowers in love. Carried away in the air, in love. Titian's nudes. Leda and the swan. A woman called Angélique. Love elevated to that level. Love scene suspended between heaven and earth, on a balcony.

Candor hardly lit, above the horizon, in that glass of air.

Laurel rose: cool brazier.

*

SEPTEMBER

Dreams. Sleep interrupted more often reveals their number, their intensity. I am struck by the distance that separates my dreams (I don't pay much attention to them, as a rule, especially because I don't often catch them) from my books. The subject matter of dreams is, deep down, that of newspapers, "bad" newspapers. Sex and violence. Garish, very often, as in a film: close-ups, obvious allegories, etc. I did notice that dreams about prisons became more frequent, for a time; I also live through spy stories in my dreams, stories with gangs, ridiculous, brutal, frightening. Dreams re-establish contact with that low common subject matter, which is also the subject matter of history, now as always.

It may very well be true that my poetry neglects these lower regions too often.

Two dreams I've written down:

A—Beginning forgotten. The story is set in a house, ours, but it doesn't look like ours. The bell rings. It's the new cleaning lady, the one we had given up on. She comes with L (our previous cleaning lady, in reality), with an escort of two dogs and two or three cats. We suggest, timidly, that they might not take to our own pets too well, but we realize we shall have to accept that. The kitchen is narrow, cluttered up with furniture and very old utensils. Suddenly a close-up of L, her thick hair undone, she holds a kitten by the ear. It screams in despair. I see that old, pink, wrinkled face, in tears. She explains that this particular cat is ill, doomed (that is what we thought of her, in reality, after we saw her in hospital, not so long ago). We get more and more annoyed. The new woman keeps smiling, unmoved.

Her three or four cats get hold of my leg, later; I can't shake them off. I get mad and fire the woman and the company she keeps.

B—I regret I lost big chunks of this dream, because I felt it must have been very beautiful, when I woke up, coherent, without a single break and not extravagant.

I am left with little: I walk, or rather I wander about in a very big and empty house; no furniture, as in the galleries or halls of certain castles. There seem to be two floors, both of one big hall, joined by a big staircase. I am struck by the size of doors and windows. No decorations. An immense void, obscure and shut up. I walk. I don't remember if I'm at ease or not. Maybe. Suddenly I see a shape as if leaning against the angle of a chimney; it looks like a bundle of clothes, at first, a kind of tweed jacket (more or less), then it rapidly dawns on me that somebody is standing there, leaning against the wall—and I find myself looking at a face only, a face that is turned away from me, the face of a woman with short hair, a redhead maybe, unknown, anyway, silent. She points at a door in the wall, somewhere in the dark, maybe with her arm, maybe just because her face is turned that way. I realize I have to follow her, or walk through that door in front of her.

That is when I woke up, not, as you might think, under the impression that I had just come out of a nightmare, but rather with the impression of a solemn, sovereign beauty. That door I had been invited to walk through might well have led to death, but also (I think that thought occurred to me in my dream or immediately afterwards) to an appetizing hell.

I remember, in this context, that I have often reminded myself, these many years, that my very first (?) dream as a child was of an immense dragon, in painted wood, in a landscape with mountains, clouds or thunderstorms. That dragon had some sort of keys on him (as of a piano) that could have been so many doors through which you could sink into him.

OCTOBER

The pink of evening. The dust, the purple, then red smoke of evening. The whole sky caught in that reflection of a distant conflagration, in that incense; scattered in pink dust. At the end of a hot day without clouds, with hunters on the hills, whistling, shouting, shooting.

There was that moment first, by the Dèves farm and the Grangette, when the earth itself and the mountain became almost transparent once again (which isn't saying much, and not saying it well), mere screens before an inner light, under a sky that was all light itself.

Then the question came back to mind: what relation, what link between death and the fact that we see, that we drink it with our eyes that wine of light.

Everything, not just the sky, has grown vaguely pink a few moments later, an ashy pink that turns to purple and blue, a slightly dark pink, therefore, tenderly grave, sparse and omnipresent like perfume.

*

Morning fog beyond the first trees. I think of Keats, the *Ode to Autumn*:

> *Season of mists and mellow fruitfulness* . . .

then of Leopardi:

> *Vaghe stelle dell'Orsa, io non credea*
> *Tornare ancor per uso a contemplarvi* . . .

Should I put extracts from critical essays in the "new" style (that of almost all literary magazines nowadays) next to these two quotations, or so many others taken from the purest products of poetry—I'm afraid there might appear a slight incompatibility.

*

I have always been very sensitive to Petrarch's Italian, even if I don't know it well, wherever I open his books again. I feel that language (immediately, before all reflexion or analysis) as totally clear cut, completely porous, as made up of sonorous openings (as if you walked through galleries all of glass and space). Sound sweet and crystalline at the same time. But above all porous, for the divine infinite. Alveoles. A web of words that holds the sky or filters it as the trees do?

Language in harmony with the Tuscan landscape; the way I thought I could *see* lines from St. John of the Cross in the landscape of Majorca, in the past.

NOVEMBER

Autumn: rain on the flames. Landscape flaming and cold. Flowers, mist, humidity. If the rain itself would burn . . .

*

A visit to the house of the deceased. A dog under the dead woman's bed; three unsightly crones by her bedside. One of them gets up from time to time to sprinkle holy water on that face of wax. In the room you have to walk through pastel-coloured underwear, with little flowers, is lying around on the bed, unmade.